Deaf Friendly Nurseries & Pre-schools:

A guide for people working with deaf children in early education settings

Who is this book for?

The purpose of this book is to provide early years workers with information and practical advice about how to meet the needs of very young deaf children, up to the age of five.

This book is specifically aimed at people working with deaf children in a range of early education settings, such as:

- nurseries

- playgroups

- opportunity groups

- parent and toddler groups

- crèches

- where a childminding service is provided

In this booklet we have used:

- the word 'nursery' to include all early education settings

- the term 'deaf' to cover all types of hearing loss, including temporary hearing loss such as glue ear

- the term 'advisory services'; however in your work you may come across the terms 'hearing impaired services' or 'sensory support services' being used

- the word 'parent' to include the child's carer with parental responsibility

Contents

Section 1

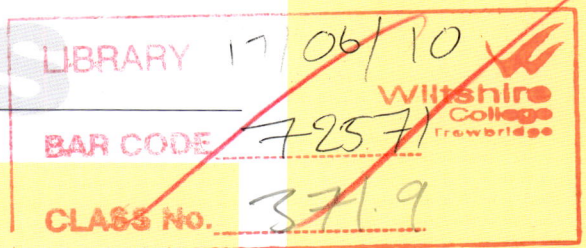

Contents

Section 1

Introduction

In a deaf friendly nursery there is a positive attitude towards deafness and deaf children are enabled and encouraged to reach their potential. In order to achieve this it is essential that all staff:

- understand the needs of deaf children

- can ensure that the environment and activities are accessible for deaf children

- know where to go for further information and advice

In this booklet we use the term 'deaf' to describe all types of hearing loss whether that loss is permanent or temporary. It is estimated that there are 25,000 deaf children in the UK with permanent deafness ranging from moderate to profound. Other children will have mild deafness and some will have a deafness that affects one ear (unilateral deafness). As many as one in five children will experience temporary deafness as a result of glue ear. (More information about the different types of deafness is given in Section 2 – *What is deafness?*).

There is no such thing as a typical deaf child. However, it is important to have an understanding of deafness and how it affects a child's learning and development.

Deafness itself is not defined as a special educational need. Nevertheless, there are needs arising from deafness, whether it is temporary or permanent, which may require special educational provision. For example, a young child's language and communication development can often be affected by their deafness, although this is not necessarily a reflection of a child's ability or potential. Deaf children may need extra provision in the form of regular speech and language

"Me deaf, me like playschool, like books, like water."

Jack, three years old

3

therapy; support from a teacher of the deaf; specialist equipment such as a radio aid system; or sign language support.

The support that a child has in the early years of their life will have a significant impact on their development. Young deaf children need to have a language-rich environment and the opportunity to learn from their peers and adults. Early years workers can ensure that young deaf children get the most out of their early education by:

- providing a range of activities that enable children to learn from each other

- allowing children time to absorb information and to observe cause and effect

- supporting children so that they feel confident and secure and able to 'take risks' with their learning

- enabling children to make connections within their learning

- encouraging a positive self-identity

Being a deaf friendly nursery is about having a holistic approach to deaf issues. This means that all polices, including those on child protection, equal opportunities and health and safety, should recognise and reflect the needs of deaf children. Staff training and professional development programmes need to include regular training on deaf awareness and working with deaf children. Parents should not only be informed about their child's development, but should also be encouraged to share their knowledge of their child, contribute to their child's learning and review their progress.

In your nursery you will already be adapting the curriculum in order to meet the diverse needs of the children. Many deaf children will need different and additional support and therefore are likely to have a Statement of Special Educational needs and/or an Individual Education Plan (IEP) (in England, Wales & Northern Ireland) or a Record of Needs and/or Individualised Education Programme (IEP) (in Scotland). Staff not only need to be aware of the contents of a child's Statement/Record or IEP, but need to know how to put this in to practice. There should be clear information about reviewing a child's progress and ensuring that their support remains appropriate. This is particularly important in the early years as a young child's needs can change over a short time. The teacher of the deaf and special educational needs co-ordinator (SENCO) or special educational needs adviser (Scotland only) will be able to give you information and advice about working with individual deaf children.

We hope that you find this booklet to be a useful resource and that you will use the information and advice to develop a truly inclusive environment where deaf children will be able to make the most of their early education before starting school. For further information or advice about any of the issues raised in this booklet, please contact The National Deaf Children's Society Freephone helpline on 0808 800 8880 (voice & text).

Welcoming a deaf child into your nursery

How do parents choose a nursery?

Parents will have their own criteria for choosing a nursery, such as:

- reputation
- whether the staff have experience of working with deaf children
- size of the classes
- suitability of the building, such as the acoustics
- general atmosphere and ethos
- behaviour of other children
- child/adult ratio
- access to deaf role models
- if there are other deaf children

Parents may have visited a number of different places before deciding which one is right for their child. For some families this may mean choosing a nursery that is outside the area where they live. Parents need to feel reassured that their child's needs will be met and that they are welcome to talk to you or other members of the staff if they ever have concerns.

Providing an introduction book or even a short video to show everyday routines in the nursery will give a deaf child and their parents an understanding of what happens during the day and whether it is suitable for their needs.

It is essential that you try to find out as much as possible about a deaf child before they start, as this will help with preparing to meet their needs. Parents will have vital information about their child. Also other people who may be familiar with the family such as their teacher of the

"The reason why I chose this nursery is because it is small and looks homely and the staff there are very welcoming. Also we had a look at the ceiling and carpet for acoustic reasons."

Mother of a deaf child

deaf, will be able to provide advice and support.

If you know that a deaf child will be starting at your nursery, then you might find it useful to arrange a visit to places which have experience of supporting deaf children, such as:

- other nurseries where there are deaf children
- a school for deaf children
- a mainstream school with a unit or resource base for deaf children

As well as this, carrying out an audit of the environment and staff skills can help to highlight areas that need to be addressed. For instance, you might need to think about changing the layout to make it more deaf friendly and arrange deaf awareness training.

Home visits

Home visits can be very useful for you and for a child's parents. When going on a home visit, it is worth taking two of you so that one person can play with the child whilst the other can focus on learning as much as possible from the child's parents. This is helpful because the person playing with the child can use the opportunity to observe some of the communication strategies that the family are using at home, such as how they use various gestures, signs or specific words to explain tasks or interpret requests. It also allows the parent time to concentrate on giving you all of the relevant information that you need to know, such as their expectations, their child's likes and dislikes, their preferred method of communication, what hearing aids they wear and how they are managed. If it is not possible to arrange a home visit, then invite parents to come and see you.

If the family members are deaf, their first language may be British Sign Language (BSL) or Irish Sign Language (ISL). If this is the case, then check with the family what communication support they want so that you can make the necessary arrangements, such as booking a sign language interpreter. This is also a consideration where a child is from a different ethnic or cultural background.

Partnership with parents

Partnership with parents is the key to ensuring that deaf children get the most out of their time in nursery. Below are some examples which parents and early years workers have identified as helping to make this partnership successful.

Advice from parents:

- be aware that different parents have different ways of coming to terms with their child's deafness

- show awareness and understanding of a deaf child's needs

- consider how a child's cultural and social needs can be met

- keep parents up-to-date with their child's development and progress

- be honest about what is or is not working

- offer ideas and suggestions about what families can do at home to support their child's learning

Suggestions from pre-school workers:

- allow parents to determine their degree of involvement in decisions affecting their child

- keep notes of your observations and the child's progress and share these with the family

- work with parents in setting realistic and achievable goals

- involve parents in planning and reviewing meetings

- invite parents to take part in nursery activities

- organise coffee mornings or other activities so that parents can get together

- know where to go for more help and advice

- be willing to share knowledge and expertise and to learn new skills

"Inclusion for us is not only giving children access to the environment; it's recognising that this can only be achieved through partnership with their parents."

Nursery nurse

The wider team

There may be a number of different professionals working with a deaf child and their family. Although you may not meet all of the people involved, it is important to be clear about each agency's role. When the family want advice or ask questions that you cannot answer, it is essential that you know who to go to for the information or which person to refer the family to. It is also essential that each agency involved with the family is aware of what the other is doing, so that families are not receiving contradictory advice.

The family may also have a key worker who co-ordinates the various agencies. The key worker is usually a qualified teacher of the deaf or early years support worker. This person will be responsible for liaising with the family to ensure good communication, clear co-operation and effective partnership of all who are involved with the family.

Below is a list of the range of people who a family may be in contact with:

- health visitor

- teacher of the deaf

- speech and language therapist

- family doctor/general practitioner (GP)

- paediatrician

- ear nose and throat (ENT) consultant

- audiologist

- nursery/playgroup leader

- special educational needs co-ordinator (SENCO) or adviser

- deaf role model/sign language tutor

- social worker for deaf people

- befriender/advocate

Communication

Communication can mean using sign language, speech or a mixture of both. Find out as much as possible about the communication method being used at home and check with parents how they want you to communicate with their child. (The different communication methods are explained in Section 2 – *Communication options*.)

It is quite possible that some parents of a young deaf child may not have yet decided on which method of communication they wish to use and are trying out everything to see what works well for their child.

Whatever method of communication the family is using at home, it is important that it is continued throughout the child's nursery education. This is so that they can benefit from learning through trying out a range of different and interesting experiences.

Some families may choose an auditory-oral approach, whilst others may choose sign language or total communication for their child and it is important that you understand how to meet their child's communication needs and develop their language. The teacher of the deaf will be able to provide you with information and advice on how to develop a range of communication skills.

Lipreading

Lipreading isn't just about reading people's lips, but also involves reading body language to pick up vital clues as to how certain words are said (in the same way that hearing people would pick up clues from listening to a speaker's intonation). As some deaf children may not be able to hear the words that are directly spoken to them, they have to learn to make sense of the shape of the words that they are introduced to. It requires intense concentration and can be very tiring. At times it is very easy to misread some words because they look similar on the mouth to other words even though they sound different, for example:

a) bat   mat   pat
b) chip   ship   trip
c) chain   train   drain

Lipreading may aid a child's listening skills as it gives some visual clues as to what a person is saying. A child will need time to get used to a person's lip patterns before they are able to lipread well enough to make sense of the words that they are using. Some people may be more difficult to lipread than others because they have an accent or dialect which a child is not familiar with.

When you talk it is important that you look at a deaf child all the time you are speaking, so that they can see what you are saying and that they are aware you are talking to them. A deaf child needs a good knowledge of written and spoken English before they are able to use lipreading effectively. You cannot lipread and understand a word that you have never seen before. So for a young child it is essential that you try to give as many visual clues as possible to make your conversation more meaningful to them. It may also be necessary to rephrase some words or sentences in order for a child to understand.

Deaf children need to develop fluent language skills in order to understand and influence the world around them, by whichever approach is the most appropriate for the individual child."

NDCS Vision
and Values

A good lipreading environment would be:

- one to two metres between the speaker and the lipreader
- good lighting so that a lipreader can see your lips clearly and to ensure that your face is not in a shadow
- providing plenty of extra clues - both visual and auditory

Things that can hinder lipreading are:

- looking away whilst talking
- mumbling and not looking directly at the lipreader
- an overgrown moustache or beard
- wearing sunglasses so that it is not possible to read the expression of your eyes
- wearing large dangling earrings which can occasionally catch the light
- standing in front of distracting wallpaper
- too many people moving behind the speaker
- talking with chewing gum or other food in your mouth
- putting your hands over your mouth whilst talking
- too many people talking at once
- using exaggerated mouth patterns as these can distort the speaking rhythm

When you change the subject in your conversation, always make sure that you let a child know; otherwise they may still be thinking about the first topic that you were talking about. As a guide it is useful to introduce the topic first before expanding on it ie "Swimming, today we are going swimming. What will we need to take with us for swimming?" It helps if the child has an idea of what you will be talking about before trying to lipread the extra information. If necessary show a picture so that they can make a connection with the words.

Sign language

If a child is using sign language, it is important that this approach can be supported in the nursery. Staff need to have appropriate sign language skills in order to communicate with a deaf child and promote their language development. As well as this, it is equally important that hearing children are able to learn sign language so that they can communicate with their deaf peers. This also reduces any potential for a deaf child to be isolated.

To develop your signing skills you can:

- enrol on a sign language class at your local college (preferably one that is focused on child and family signs)

- find out if there are any classes in your local area especially for parents of young deaf children which you can take part in

- contact local units or schools for deaf children to see if they have a sign language tutor or communication support worker who could provide training

- ask the advisory service for advice and training

Deaf role models

Deaf adults have an important part to play in the inclusion of deaf children in early education settings. Not only can they provide a young deaf child with a role model, they can also support their language acquisition, encourage the use of different communication strategies and foster personal and social development. Therefore, it is important to make sure that those deaf adults who work in the nursery or visit on a regular basis, are included in planning activities and reviewing a child's progress. As well as working directly with children, deaf adults can also help staff by providing advice and delivering deaf awareness training and sign language tuition.

"Watching deaf and hearing children sign together is great, it makes my job worthwhile."

Deaf role model

"One of the most interesting things about my job is being there to answer the questions the children have about being deaf. I think it's good for young deaf children to be able to have contact with deaf adults and older deaf children."

Deaf role model

General hints and tips on communicating with a deaf child

The following is just a sample of what can be done to help support a young deaf child in a nursery whether they are using speech/lipreading, sign language or a mixture of both (please also see the previous section on lipreading):

- make sure that you have a child's attention before starting a conversation

- always get down to a child's eye level

- make sure the room is well lit and that you don't have your back to a window, as this creates a shadow making it difficult to read facial expressions or lipread

- arrange the seating so that all children can see you and each other

- be within a good distance so that they can see or hear you

- listening and lipreading are very tiring so don't overload the child with too many oral instructions

- remember your voice is not the only sound being heard, as there may be additional sounds being amplified through hearing aids/a cochlear implant

- try to encourage other children to speak one at a time and to be aware of noise levels

- if a child is using sign language, make sure that your handshapes are clear

- if a child is not using sign language, still use your hands and facial expressions to gesture and support what you are saying

- give as many visual clues as possible, for example bring the appropriate object or toy near to your face so that they can make the connection to what you are referring to

- let a child know when you are going to change the topic of the conversation

- check that a child has understood you – if they haven't, you may need to rephrase a sentence or use a different word or sign

- never shout as it will distort your facial expression and it will make it harder for a child to lipread

- even when children are not using words, we can recognise their feelings or needs by observing their:

  - focus of attention

  - facial expression

  - body language

An inclusive environment

The design and layout of the environment can have a significant impact on learning and for deaf children this can mean the difference between being included or excluded in activities.

Have a good look around the nursery and pinpoint the busiest parts and the quietest parts of the room. It can be very difficult for a deaf child to concentrate on listening to different sounds if the environment is very noisy. A deaf child may be wearing their hearing aids or have a cochlear implant and it can be quite distressing or frightening if there are sudden loud noises, such as the screeching of chairs being dragged across the floor. Some nurseries are held in buildings where the acoustics are poor and for someone who has to wear hearing aids, sounds can echo or be distorted. Listening conditions can be improved by:

- fitting blinds or curtains
- carpeting floors
- using wall displays and tablecloths to cover and soften large flat surfaces
- closing the window or door when there is a noise outside

Where are the windows? Remember a child cannot see your face well if you are standing in front of the light or a window. For activities or group work it might be better for a deaf child to be placed with their back to the window so that they can see you, the other children and be aware of what is happening in the room.

What is the quiet corner like? Are there too many distracting pictures around? Put colourful pictures and posters a bit higher, above a child's eye level so that they can concentrate on looking at you rather than being distracted by the pictures/posters.

Activity tables or places where there is a high level of interaction, such as water play areas, have the potential for language development. Look at where they can be placed so that a deaf child is not distracted by what is going on around them.

What about the book corner? Include books with pictures of children wearing hearing aids or cochlear implants and that feature sign language in the stories. This is particularly useful if a child and their family are using signs at home. It is equally important to have some simple books which explain about deafness for the other children to look at.

It may not be possible to alter everything; however making specific changes to the environment can help to make it more deaf friendly. Remember it may not just be deaf children who will benefit, but also those who do not have good communication skills or who are not very confident.

Inclusive learning strategies

To ensure that deaf children are fully included within the life of a nursery and that they have the same access to learning as other children, you may need to make changes to the way you plan and carry out activities. Below are some examples of good practice when working with pre-school age deaf children.

Home communication book

A home/nursery communication book can be an effective way for parents and nursery staff to share news about what a child has been doing. Examples of a child's work, and a list of words or signs they have been learning could be included so that their parents can follow this up at home. The book can also be used by a child as a prompt when telling their parents about their day.

Additionally, parents can write about what they have been doing with their child at home and pass on important information, such as if they have an audiology appointment. This can then be explored at nursery through role-playing or reading a book on the topic, as a way of helping a child to prepare.

Registration

When taking the register, you can ask children to fingerspell their names or to sign their names (if they know how to do that), or ask them to stand up so that a deaf child will get to know who is who.

My name is Curtis

C

Using sign names is a good way for children to learn their friends' names, as it can be a bit daunting to remember everyone's name. Teach children how to make up their own sign name; it could be related to a particular interest such as Tom (train), Abigail (ponytail), Meena (flower), and Mrs Marsh (glasses). Alternatively teach them to fingerspell the initial letter of their name and have a poster of fingerspelling up on the wall. Encourage children to sign each others name when you want them to do certain things, but bear in mind that some fingerspelling letters can be difficult to form and some of the vowel sounds can be confusing, especially if their hand-eye co-ordination is not well developed.

Perhaps have a large card with the initial letters and ask children to put up their hands if their name begins with a certain letter. It can be a fun way of getting them to recognise the alphabet.

For free copies of fingerspelling posters or postcards (British Sign Language only) please contact the NDCS.

Social communication and independence

It is important to provide opportunities for a deaf child to develop their communication skills. Some deaf children may be reluctant to join in with others and will need a lot of encouragement to take part in games and activities. It may be necessary to build up their confidence, but always in a way that is appropriate to their level of development. Other children will want to take their own lead.

Activity time is a good opportunity to observe a child and to see how they are communicating and learning as they carry out a task. There are

Why don't you join in?

a range of strategies you can use to check out their understanding, such as asking questions. Don't be afraid to ask again if you are not sure what they meant by their answer because the more you interact the more you will start to understand their way of thinking.

Here are some tips to try out:

- observe a deaf child with their parent or with a deaf adult to see how they interact

- allow a child time to finish a task before trying to engage their attention, otherwise they may still be thinking about what they were doing before

- involve a third person/object, such as a teddy or a doll and ask if the teddy/doll wants a drink

- ask them to repeat what they are trying to convey if they are not clear about telling something

- tell them to quieten down or to speak a bit louder if they are talking too loudly or too quietly

- encourage them to use their hearing aids/cochlear implant and to let you know if they are working or not

- when they are not very familiar with certain words, do check their understanding

- try to include other children too so that they are aware of how to engage a deaf child's attentions; for example, if a child has missed a flashing light or instruction because they are engrossed in a task, then encourage the other children to tap them on the shoulder so that they know what is happening

Ellie, please tap Sharmila on the shoulder to get her attention, thank you.

Visual clues and toys

Having photographs of adults with their names underneath can help children to learn who is who. Visual diaries that have signs with written text and a pictorial clue can help children to learn routines and to know what to expect. This can also be used for different tasks such as tidying up, washing hands or hanging up coats.

Remember to use toys which are not beyond the child's level of language and choose toys which are brightly coloured, feel nice to touch, have an interesting texture and/or are attractive to look at.

Monday	Tuesday	Wednesday	Thursday	Friday
Play time	Story Time	Cooking	Farm Trip	Play time
Music Time	Painting	Story Time	Farm Trip	Story Time

Reading books

When reading a book with a deaf child think about the seating arrangement; for instance try and sit face to face or slightly sideways. You also need to be within touching distance so that you can touch them to gain their attention from time to time. Like all children they need time to look at pictures and to absorb the information.

It is a good idea to look at books beforehand to see if the pictures alone can make sense; some pictures may be a bit fuzzy or have too much detail which makes it difficult for a child to follow the main character through the story. Do use a lot of facial expressions and ask questions such as "What do you think will happen next?"

Story time

At story time think about the story book that you will be using with the children. Are the pictures visual enough to make sense of what the story is about? It might be a good idea to let a deaf child have a look at the book so that they have some idea of the sequence of the story.

When telling a story:

- use different props and visual clues to help explain what is happening

- use a lot of facial expression to show the humour or the different moods of the characters

- if a child is learning sign language then use signs to go with the words in the story - it will be fun for other children to learn the new signs and reinforce their learning of new words too

- encourage children to act out parts of the story

- include some deaf awareness, for example, some of the characters could be deaf such as a deaf granddad who knew someone was at the door because of the flashing door bell

Group time

At group time try and remember the following points to make it easier for the deaf child to feel included:

- first, get all of the children to sit in a circle so that everyone can see each other

- when asking questions, make sure that a deaf child is aware of who is speaking

- try to make sure that each child takes turns in talking so that a deaf child can try and lipread them one at a time

- be aware of the noise level - play a game of putting your hand up or down so that children will know that they have to be quiet, because it will be difficult for a deaf child to hear what is going on if too many children are talking at once

- if a deaf child is using a radio aid, make sure that whoever is speaking has the radio aid microphone on. However, if it isn't possible for the children to pass the radio aid to one another when they speak, repeat what has been said (for further information on radio aids please see Section 2 – *Technical support*)

- remember to have some visual props ready to explain what the topic is about

Music time

Music is a good way of encouraging a child to listen to different sounds. If possible find a quiet area so that a deaf child can try instruments and experience the sounds and vibrations. A vibration box is good fun for children as they can feel the different vibrations. If you don't have one of these, ask the teacher of the deaf if they know where you could borrow one from.

During music time use action songs so that everyone can join in. Remember that a deaf child might need visual clues to follow what is happening, such as when to join in or when the music has stopped.

Playing games

This is best done in a small group as you will need to explain how the rules work and, if necessary, you can use another child or an adult to demonstrate how things should be done. There are a lot of games that children can play to develop their communication and social skills. These are some ideas:

- imagination games such as imitating different animals and getting other children to guess

- facial expression games to demonstrate the different moods of the characters in the story

- games which can help to develop observation skills, such as putting different coloured cards around the room and when you sign or say the name of the colour they have to go to the right one

Preparing for an outing

It is important to prepare a deaf child for an outing so that they can experience the anticipation like the other children. This can be done by:

- using pictures
- having different objects that are related to the visit on the interest table with books explaining the topic
- using one to one time to explain the new vocabulary

Behaviour and discipline

Like all children, deaf children need to learn what is and is not acceptable. Do not allow a deaf child to get away with things that you would not let other children do. It will become harder and more confusing if a child does not understand and believes that they can get away with things. Here are some suggestions:

- if they get upset let them calm down before attempting to get their eye contact
- if they refuse to look at you, be patient and stay with them
- explain why they were not allowed to do what they wanted
- use examples of when they, or other children, have been good and explain why
- use the opportunity to talk about feelings so that they can become aware of different emotions

Understanding deafness

How to identify deafness

If you have concerns about a child's hearing it is important to raise them with their parents. Parents should be encouraged to visit their family doctor (GP) and to make sure that if deafness is suspected the child is referred for further tests.

The following may indicate a potential deafness:

- does not respond when called

- a delay in learning to speak

- a lack of clarity in speech, slurring of words, incorrect pronunciation

- unstressed words in speech (especially prepositions eg 'in', 'on', 'up') may be missed or misinterpreted

- watches the face/lips intently

- reluctant to speak freely, eg a nod or shake of the head rather than saying 'yes' or 'no'

- displays of inappropriate behaviour or temper tantrums

- verb tenses may be incorrect

- any difficulty in listening and attending to speech

- constantly asking for repetition - 'pardon?', 'what?', 'eh?'
- failure to follow instructions straight away or misunderstands/ignores instructions
- requires repeated explanations
- watches what the others are doing before doing it themselves
- continues with an activity when the rest of the class has stopped
- inattentive and 'daydreaming'
- doesn't pick up information from overheard conversations
- attempts to control and dominate conversation through talking
- becomes withdrawn
- makes little or no contribution to group discussions
- shouts, or talks overly loudly
- speaks very softly
- complains of not being able to hear
- frequently seeks assistance from peers

What is deafness?

Some children are born deaf, and other children may become deaf later on due to, for example, an illness. There are two main types of deafness, which are described below:

Conductive deafness

This is the most common type of deafness. It means that sounds cannot pass through the outer and middle ear to the cochlea and auditory nerve in the inner ear. This is often caused by fluid in the middle ear (glue ear). **Children under the age of 5 are the largest group affected by glue ear.** Glue ear can cause temporary deafness and can either clear up naturally after a short period of time, or it can develop into a long-term condition requiring surgical intervention or lead to a child wearing a hearing aid.

Sensori-neural deafness or nerve deafness

As sound passes through the outer and middle ear, tiny hair cells in the cochlea convert sound waves into electrical signals. These signals travel along the nerve of hearing, (the auditory nerve) to the brain. Most cases of sensori-neural deafness are caused by loss of, or damage, to the hair cells in the cochlea which means that the cochlea is not processing the sound effectively. Deafness may be passed down in families even if there is no apparent history of deafness. It can also be caused by an infectious disease such as rubella, mumps, measles, or meningitis. A child may be born deaf because of a shortage of oxygen in the bloodstream at birth or some other birth trauma.

The term 'mixed deafness' is often used when a child has a mixture of conductive and sensori-neural deafness.

There are different degrees of deafness and these are most often classified as mild, moderate, severe or profound. Few children are totally deaf. Most deaf children can hear some sounds at certain pitches and volume. Deaf children with the same level of deafness may experience sounds differently. There are some children who have little or no hearing in one ear, and ordinary levels of hearing in the other. This is known as unilateral deafness.

To give some idea of what some deaf children can hear please see the diagram below. Also listed are the degrees of deafness. It is important to be aware that children who wear hearing aids/a cochlear implant may be able to access more sounds. This will vary from child to child.

For further information about deafness please contact the NDCS for a copy of the booklet *Understanding Deafness*. The NDCS also has information on glue ear and meningitis and deafness.

A visual representation of the loudness and pitch of a range of everyday sounds.

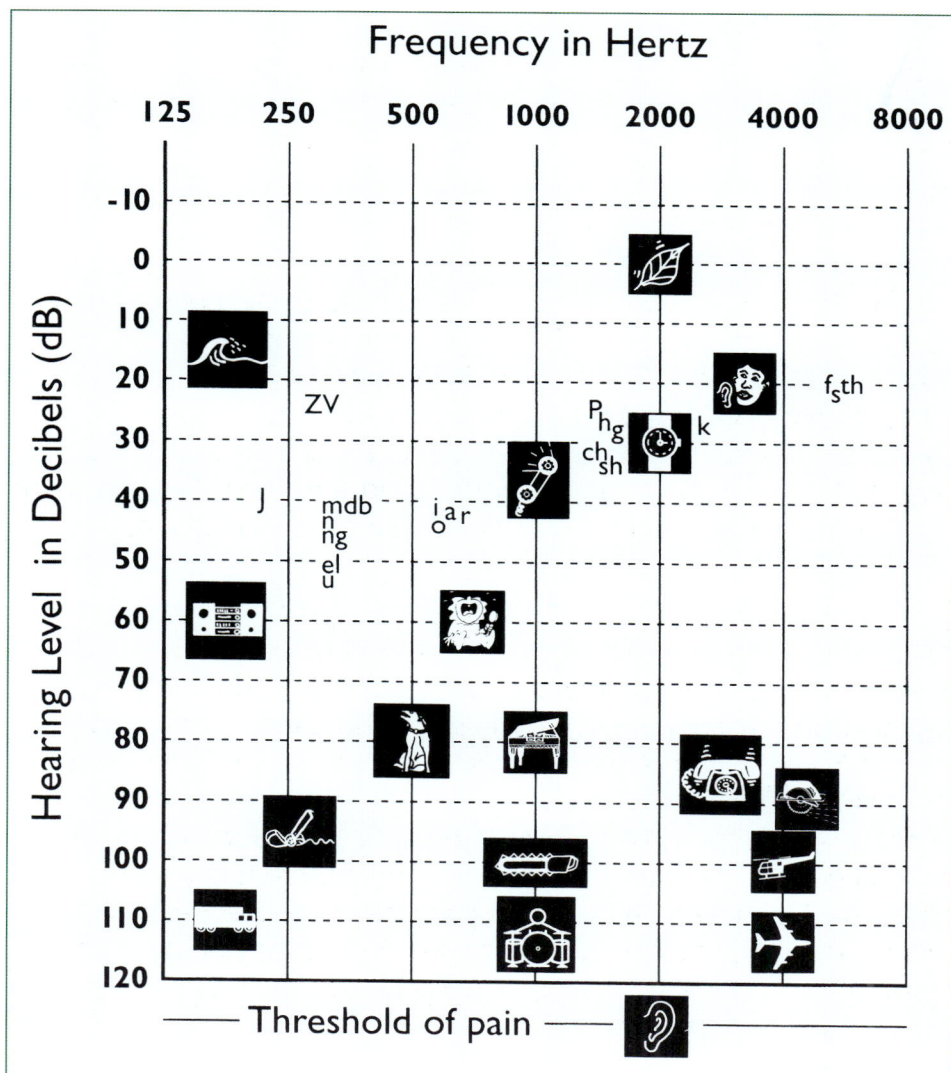

Mild deafness
20 - 40 dB

Moderate deafness
41 - 70 dB

Severe deafness
71 - 95 dB

Profound deafness
95+ dB

(Source: British Society of Audiology 1988)

Communication options

Choosing which method of communication their deaf child will use is a difficult decision for many parents. There is no correct answer, and there is widespread debate as to which communication methods are preferable. The National Deaf Children's Society believes in informed choice and that as all children are different, it is important that the chosen communication method meets the individual child's needs. It is equally important that the child is comfortable with the communication method provided, so where possible a deaf child should be consulted as to which method of communication they prefer. There are a number of different communication options. The three main communication methods are **auditory-oral approaches, sign bilingualism** and **total communication (TC).**

Auditory-oral approaches

All auditory-oral approaches maintain that, with the use of hearing aids, radio aids and cochlear implants to amplify residual hearing, children can develop their listening skills and so a spoken language. These approaches are used with children who may have deafness ranging from mild to profound. Auditory-oral approaches do not use sign language or fingerspelling to support the understanding of spoken language. There are differences between the types of approach and the direction of support and intervention.

The **natural aural approach** is the most widely used of the auditory-oral approaches. It emphasizes the role of the family in helping deaf children to develop spoken language naturally, as a result of the normal experiences of childhood and based on the consistent use of well-maintained hearing aids or cochlear implants. The **structured oral approach** is slightly different. It is used to encourage the child to develop speech and language, using residual hearing and lipreading and a particular structured teaching system. It often uses written language to lend support to the learning process. You may also come across other types of auditory-oral approaches, such as **maternal reflective** and **auditory verbal therapy (AVT).**

Lipreading (sometimes referred to as **speechreading**) is the ability to read lip patterns. Lipreading is difficult to learn, but many deaf children will naturally try to lipread when they are communicating. However it would be very difficult for most deaf children to rely solely on lipreading to communicate, as they can only pick up a small percentage of what is being said. It also requires intense and sustained concentration; this means it can be very tiring. So lipreading would usually be used in line with other communication approaches (please see Section 1 - *Communication* for further information on lipreading).

Sign bilingualism

This essentially describes an approach that systematically encourages the learning and using of two languages at one time, a sign language and a spoken/written language. In Britain, for deaf children, these are English (or another spoken language) and British Sign Language (BSL) or Irish Sign Language (ISL), either one being the preferred language of the child. The assumption behind this approach is that if parents are given the right support and encouragement, they can learn to communicate with their deaf child. Many parents prefer to use their first language, eg English, Welsh or Urdu, with their child. This can be in spoken form or spoken with signs taken from BSL/ISL (known as Sign Supported English). Bilingualism encourages this. However, it is also seen to be important that a child has access to adults using both BSL/ISL and English. This means that a child will have access to both the language used by their parents and deaf adults whose native language is BSL/ISL. The majority of deaf children are born to hearing parents, so it is felt important that parents should be given the opportunity to meet deaf adults to learn and see sign language in a positive way.

British Sign Language (BSL) and **Irish Sign Language (ISL)** are used by over 70,000 people within the British Deaf Community. They are visual languages using hand-shapes, facial expressions, gestures and body language to communicate. Independent and complete languages with unique vocabulary, they have a structure and grammar different from that of written and spoken English or Irish. In common with other languages, they have evolved over time and developed regional dialects.

For further information on sign language please contact the NDCS for a copy of the booklet *Sign language and your deaf child*.

Fingerspelling is where each letter of the alphabet is given its own sign. It is used for signing names and places, or for a word that doesn't have a sign.

Total communication

Total communication (TC) is a philosophy that involves selecting the communication method(s) most appropriate for a deaf child at any one time. The idea behind this approach is that sign language will not replace but support the use of the oral method of communication and the use of any residual hearing, to help the development of speech and language skills. The most common sign language systems used in this approach are **Signed English (SE)** or **Sign Supported English (SSE)**, which both take signs from BSL and use fingerspelling. SE, designed as a teaching tool, is where a sign is used for every spoken word in English word order. Its aim is to develop reading and writing skills. SSE is again used in English word order but does not attempt to sign every word that is spoken.

Other sign systems such as **Cued Speech** and **Signalong** may also be used. Cued Speech is used because some words which sound different to hearing people, can look very similar when they are lipread by deaf people, eg pat and bat. It uses eight handshapes placed near the mouth to accompany spoken language to help make every sound and word clear to a deaf child. Signalong is a sign system used with children and adults who have language difficulties associated with learning disabilities and autism. It is sometimes used with deaf children. The signs are based on BSL and are used in English word order.

Makaton is a sign system that is used with children and adults (deaf and hearing), who have severe communication and learning disabilities. It uses speech, together with signs (taken from BSL) and symbols, and is grammar-free.

For further information relating to communication issues please contact the NDCS for the factsheet *Communication with deaf children and young people*. This includes a list of relevant resources.

Technical support

It is advisable to contact the local advisory service or the visiting teacher of the deaf for further details regarding technical support for an individual deaf child. The following is an example of what is available:

Hearing aids

Most hearing aids have a common purpose – to amplify sound signals. They come in various shapes and types, and may be worn on the body, behind the ear, or in the ear. Hearing aids should be adjusted by an audiologist to suit a child's specific needs. They enable people to make the most of any residual hearing they may have. They do not restore typical hearing levels. It is important to remember all noise, including background noise, is amplified making communication difficult in noisy environments.

In general, hearing aids have three main functions:

INPUT   To receive sound signals

AMPLIFICATION   To the most suitable level for the user

OUTPUT   To send the amplified sound signals to the user

This is shown in the diagram below

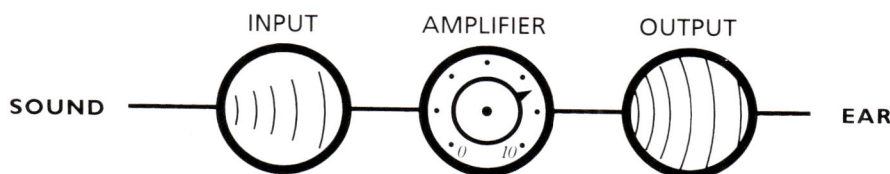

Behind the ear aid

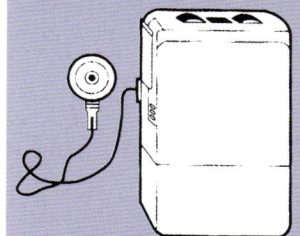

Body worn aid

In the ear aid

It is important that deafness is diagnosed as early as possible so that children can be fitted with appropriate hearing aids, which will amplify sounds to help them acquire language. It is the responsibility of the clinician concerned to provide children with the most appropriate hearing aid/s to meet their individual needs.

It can be common to find a different level of deafness in each ear. To help with this, different makes and models of hearing aids can be fitted for the left and right ears. If a child removes their hearing aids it is important to make sure that they are put back the correct way round.

Always ask the child how the aid is sounding and encourage them to tell you of any changes. It is a good idea to keep a supply of batteries for emergencies.

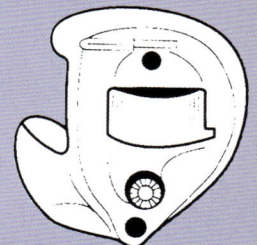

Bone conduction aid

For more information on hearing aids please contact the NDCS for a copy of the booklet *Hearing Aids: A Guide*.

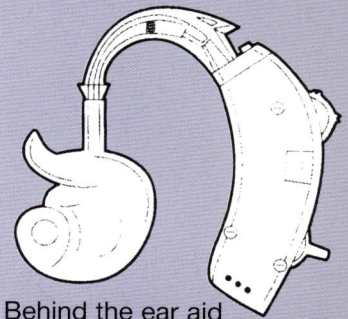

Bone anchored aid

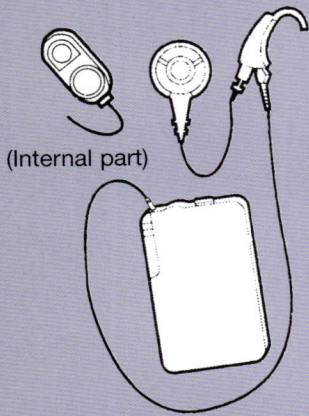

Cochlear implant

(Internal part)

Post-aural
cochlear implant

Cochlear implants

The loss of or damage to the tiny hair cells in the cochlea causes most sensori-neural deafness. Where enough functioning hair cells remain, conventional hearing aids may help. If a child has a severe to profound deafness, there may not be sufficient functioning hair cells for hearing aids to be effective. For these children a cochlear implant may be considered.

The implant is another type of hearing aid; however, instead of amplifying sound, cochlear implants send electrical signals directly to the auditory nerve. The implant bypasses the damaged hair cells in the cochlea (that cannot be stimulated by conventional hearing aids), to provide a sensation of hearing. Like hearing aids, cochlear implants do not restore typical hearing levels. The implant system has two parts. The external part consists of the speech processor (sometimes worn on the waist or behind the ear), a transmitter coil and a microphone. The internal part is surgically implanted under the skin behind the ear. It includes a number of electrodes that directly stimulate the auditory nerve.

Children who have cochlear implants can take part in most activities, though there may be exceptions. It is advisable that parents of a child with an implant check with the cochlear implant team as to which activities they can safely take part in.

For more information on cochlear implants please contact the NDCS for a copy of the leaflet or booklet *Deaf children and cochlear implants.*

Some general points in relation to hearing aids and cochlear implants

When working with deaf children who wear hearing aids or cochlear implants, it is a good idea to check that their hearing aids or cochlear implant are switched on and working before starting an activity. It is also important, for both hearing aid and cochlear implant users, that background noise is kept to a minimum. One problem that can occur with hearing aids is acoustic feedback which causes a high pitched whistling sound (usually as a result of a poor fitting earmould). You also need to be aware of the possibility that a battery may fail at any time, so it is useful to have spare batteries (this applies to cochlear implants as well as hearing aids).

Radio aids

Deaf children can wear a radio aid system together with their hearing aids or cochlear implant. A radio aid will help them to pick out the speaker's voice and cut out background noise.

Most radio aids are of a type known as 'personal systems'. These are used together with the child's hearing aids or cochlear implants. (There is one make of radio aid that has a hearing aid built into it. It uses special earpieces with earmoulds. The child does not need an ordinary hearing aid when using this radio hearing aid.)

All radio aids have two main parts: the transmitter and the receiver. The teacher wears the transmitter. A microphone picks up the teacher's voice. The sounds are then transmitted by radio waves to the receiver. The deaf child wears the receiver. This picks up the radio signal from the transmitter and converts it back to sound, which is amplified by the child's hearing aids or implant.

Radio aids work on different frequencies, like tuning into different radio stations. For example, each school class might have its own frequency so that it does not interfere with the class next door. The frequency can usually be altered quite easily, either with a control on the aid or by replacing a plug-in module. A colour, letter or number code is used to show which frequency the radio aid is working on. The transmitter and receiver must have the same code if they are to work together.

The user can receive the sound in two ways: through a neck loop or by 'direct connection' to the child's hearing aids.

A neck loop can be worn over or under the clothes. This loop is connected to the radio aid receiver by a thin lead. The child's hearing aid must be switched to the 'T' setting. This system only picks up sound from the transmitter so background noises near the child will be reduced. Most personal systems have a built-in microphone that can be switched on to pick up nearby sounds and the child's own voice. Using a neck loop can cause difficulties. Interference can be a problem and the quality of sound can vary.

Most children use 'direct connection'. The radio aid receiver is linked to the child's behind the ear hearing aid directly by a lead. The lead is attached to the hearing aid with a 'shoe'. A double, Y shaped lead can be used if the child wears two hearing aids. A small number of in the ear hearing aids also have a direct input facility. Using direct input means that both nearby sounds and the child's own voice will be picked up. This type of radio aid can be worn either on the chest or on a waist belt. A behind the ear radio aid receiver is entirely housed within a 'shoe' which slips over the end of the hearing aid. This means there is no body worn receiver and no wires.

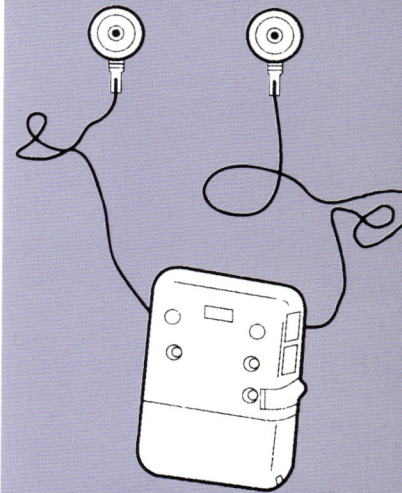

Radio aid with built-in hearing aid

Body worn radio aid receiver

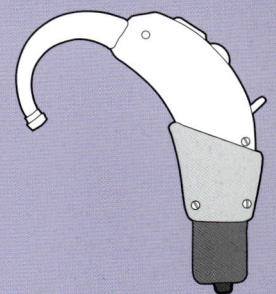

Behind the ear radio aid receiver

Basic rules to remember when using radio aids:

- although a child is using a radio aid, they may still be making use of other forms of communication, eg signing, lipreading and other visual clues

- remember to switch on the transmitter when using it to talk to a deaf child

- remember that if the radio aid transmitter is not switched off, children may be able to hear conversations that they are not supposed to hear

- a radio aid transmitter can pick up unwanted background noise - if you are standing in a particularly noisy area or if there is a sudden and unexpected noise, consider turning off the transmitter until it is quieter

- avoid wearing loose jewellery, tie-clips, etc that can knock the radio aid microphone and create noise

- radio aids must be checked regularly to make sure that they are working properly

- when using a radio aid transmitter do not fiddle with or tap into the microphone

- do not shout into the microphone

- wear the microphone approximately 15-20cm from the mouth

Soundfield systems

The soundfield system works on a similar principle to radio aids but the two pieces of equipment should not be confused. The advantage of this system is that although the speaker must still wear the microphone, there is no wiring which means both the speaker and the deaf child are able to move more freely around the room. Loudspeakers are installed around the room. Unlike a public address system, its aim is to produce a clear and consistent level of sound.

Those children who are most likely to benefit from a soundfield system are those with mild deafness who may otherwise have been given no additional support at nursery. This could include children who have temporary deafness caused for example by glue ear. For children with moderate to profound deafness, a radio aid is likely to be a better solution. Portable, desktop soundfield systems are also available that can be taken from room to room to benefit small groups of children. Children who cannot wear conventional hearing aids, or who have unilateral deafness, may benefit from a portable soundfield system.

For further information on radio aids or soundfield systems please contact the NDCS for a copy of the booklet *Radio Aids: An introductory guide for parents and teachers.*

If you have any questions about a child's radio aid, hearing aids or cochlear implant, or a soundfield system ask for advice from the visiting teacher of the deaf (from the local advisory service) or the child's parents.

The NDCS Technology Service

There is a range of technology available, such as video recorders that record subtitles and text telephones that can help deaf children in nurseries. The National Deaf Children's Society Blue Peter loan service gives children the opportunity to try out new equipment such as radio aids at home and at school.

For further details on technology available and the loan service please contact the NDCS Technology Team via the NDCS Freephone helpline or e-mail on technology@ndcs.org.uk.